Network Your Business to Prosperity

How to Use 'Know, Like and Trust' to Expand Your Business, Get New Customers and Increase Your Income

Business Professional Series #8

Richard G Lowe, Jr

Network Your Business to Prosperity

How to Use 'Know, Like and Trust' to Expand Your
Business, Get New Customers and Increase Your Income

Business Professional Series #8

Published by The Writing King
www.thewritingking.com

Network Your Business to Prosperity

Cover Artist: theamateurzone

Library of Congress Control Number:

ASIN:
ISBN: 978-1-946458-06-3 (Hardcover)
ISBN: 978-1-946458-05-6 (Paperback)
ISBN: 978-1-946458-04-9 (eBook)

Foreword

Hi! I'm Mark O'Donnell, President of RGA Network, one of the largest business networking organizations in Florida. I founded RGA to provide a casual, open place for like-minded business people to meet, and learn to know, like and trust one another so they can refer each other business.

I met Richard a year ago, at an RGA meeting. Shortly after, someone in the group needed their LinkedIn profile updated, so I referred him to Richard. I checked back a week later, and the guy was ecstatic about the service he received! Richard answered his questions and helped him make a better profile. That's a great referral experience!

It's an honor to write the forward for this great new book. Read it and you'll learn why networking is vital to expand your business, how to network, and what to avoid doing if you want to be respected and receive a steady flow of referrals.

What was my honest opinion? As I told Richard immediately after reading the book:

Holy cow – GREAT job on the book!

For 33 years, Richard was an executive at several companies, including Trader Joe's, and he learned how to network through experience. I like the way he shows, through his own eyes, how networking helped his career and the areas he managed.

Mark O'Donnell
President, RGA Network

Table of Contents

Foreword i

Table of Contents iii

Preface v

Introduction.. ix

What is Networking? 1

It's About Relationships 9

Know, Like and Trust.. 15

Networking Is Not Sales 21

How Can I Help? 27

It's Not About You 33

Act Professional 37

The Networking Meeting.. 41

Social Media... 47

Virtual Networking 53

Conclusion.. 57

Bonus: Interview with Mark O'Donnell....................... 61

About the Author 81

Books by Richard G Lowe Jr. 85

Additional Resources 91

Premium Writing Services 93

Preface

Throughout my career, I have networked with professionals all over the world. I never really thought of it as networking; it was just something that I did naturally to be able to accomplish my job.

Networking became especially important to me during my 20-year tenure as the Director of Technical Services and Computer Operations for Trader Joe's. In that position, I was directly responsible for the computing resources for a company which grossed over $15 billion dollars a year.

Company policy severely restricted the number of staff that could be hired in the office, including the IT department. To support the environment, I maintained a network of several hundred people to fill in the gaps of knowledge and skills, and help when necessary.

Networks require work – they don't just create themselves, and they tend to lose focus if they are not constantly maintained. Thus, I made the effort to call or email each person in my network on a weekly, monthly or at least quarterly basis.

However, networks don't just require communication; they require an unconditional exchange. By this I mean you must be willing to give without expectation of any return from any specific person.

Preface

Sometimes the exchange would be very simple, as when someone needed a technical manual or had a question about how to do something.

However, the exchange can get more complicated, such as when I talked with one of my networking friends long into the night about how to recover from a system crash.

My experience with business networking taught me three basic facts:

- Networking requires effort to establish contacts and keep them fresh.
- You must communicate with your networking partners regularly or the network will die.
- The willingness to give without expectation of return is the glue that makes networking succeed.

In other words, you must meet people, stay in contact with them, and give them help when needed. If you do those three things, you'll find, as I did, that, when you reach out for help, your network will respond.

When I retired from Trader Joe's a few years ago to become a professional writer, the networking skills that I had learned were essential for my success.

Upon reaching Florida, I located writing critique groups, libraries, and professional associations devoted to being an author, self-publisher, and book promoter. Additionally, I joined about a dozen online (virtual) networking groups to take advantage of writing resources all over the planet.

Being active in these groups is one of the pillars of my success as a self-published author. Without networking, it's not possible to build a business of any size or endurance.

One of the main reasons why businesses don't expand, or at least find it difficult to grow, is that they don't network effectively. They either don't do it at all, or they network incorrectly, which can even be worse than doing nothing.

I decided I had a responsibility to write this book to help business owners understand how to network. For example, I've seen many self-published authors struggle to sell their books, wondering why month after month goes by without a single purchase, when all they need to do is build their network of fans, writers and business associates. Hopefully, this book will help them, and people from any other business, understand how to leverage the power of networks to achieve their goals.

This book summarizes the techniques that I learned over the last four decades or so, combined with knowledge gained from interviewing Mark O'Donnell, president of RGA Network, Melissa Mabe, a co-director of RGA Network, Chuck Bryant, and Ron Sukenick, one of the founders of BNI, the largest business networking group in the United States.

I hope you find this information valuable, and can use it to grow your network, expand your business, and prosper.

Introduction

As I was going through school, all the way to college, and into my career, I was introverted and more or less did everything on my own, only asking for help when it was absolutely essential. Since I'd never taken the time to build relationships with teachers and administrators, when I asked for help, they didn't know, like or trust me. This made it more difficult than necessary to get things done.

Nonetheless, I did well, and got hired straight out of college by a small startup company – I was their first employee. In hindsight, that was my first success from networking, although I didn't know it at the time.

I was very busy going through college and working three jobs, along with a two hour commute each day. My best friend at the time, Don, and I both did our assignments in the computer lab in college, and unbeknownst to us at the time, we were being observed by the department head, Mr. James.

Our computer teacher was a man named Frederick – we knew him as Fred and he was 7 feet tall – who started a company called Software Techniques to help businesses install and operate their computers. In those days, computers took up entire air-conditioned rooms and disk drives were the size of washing machines.

Based on the recommendation of Mr. James, Don received a small stipend, a few hundred dollars, to attend what was, at the time, the most important computer convention in the industry. He didn't want to go alone, so he invited me to come along. I had no idea what this was about, but since he was paying for everything out of the money he received, I agreed to go with him.

During that convention, I met several of the heavyweights in the computer industry of the time. Our teacher, Fred, was one of the speakers, and invited Don and I to go to dinner with both of his partners and four of the top computer people in the late 1970s and early 80s. These were the guys who designed the first programming languages for Digital Equipment Corporation, and all of them were famous throughout the industry.

This dinner was the first time that I networked with influencers, and it made quite an impression on me. I must've made an impression on Fred, as well, because a month later I received a job offer out of the blue to come work for him as his first employee.

Later, I found out from one of his partners that Mr. James had recommended me over all the other students in his department. As a result, Fred had been watching my progress for some time, and further based upon the recommendations and insights of the people at the table during that dinner at the convention, he decided to hire me.

Because of that fateful lunch meeting, which lasted about three hours, the entire direction of my life changed. It's only from my more mature and knowledgeable viewpoint, 40 years later that I understand what happened during that brief time.

That small amount of networking, which I didn't realize was happening, resulted in some quick decisions that affected the rest of my future. Within three days of accepting the offer, I dropped out of college, moved 100 miles to a new city, and started my career in the computer industry.

Within a year, I was the Vice President of Consulting of that company, later became the Vice President of Consulting for Beck Computer Systems, and eventually wound up as the Director of Technical Services and Computer Operations at Trader Joe's. I remained there for 20 years until I decided to retire to become a professional writer.

When I started my computer career I made no attempts at business networking due to shyness and introversion, as well as a complete lack of social skills. I didn't even follow up with the heavyweights from that luncheon.

After a few years, my attitude began to change because of two factors. First, my boss was a strong proponent of networking and pushed me in that direction by using his own example to show me how it could be of benefit. Second, the job that I had to perform was so large that I was forced out of my shell to delegate, manage, and lead people, and, eventually, to reach out to people for help and advice.

As I expanded my network and built relationships, I noticed that it began to get easier to get things done. Instead of trying to do everything on my own, I was engaging with other talented and knowledgeable people who knew, liked, and trusted me and thus were eager to help. That network came in handy many times during my career, especially when I decided to look for new employment.

Introduction

Because of that journey, I have a unique viewpoint on the difference between using networking effectively and not taking advantage of building relationships at all.

The purpose of this book is to relay those lessons to you, so that you understand the concept of networking; how it can be helpful to you, your career and your business, and some of the pitfalls to watch out for in your quest to build relationships.

Mark O'Donnell, the president of RGA networks, and Melissa Mabe, Co-Director, have contributed immensely to the creation of this book by their example of the use of networking skills, and their knowledge, help, and friendship.

Much of this book is based on interviews and discussions with Mark, Melissa, Chuck Bryant, and Ron Sukenick, the president and founder of The Relationship Strategies Institute and one of the original founders of what became BNI.

By reading this book, you'll learn the secrets of networking, which will give you the tools you need to catapult yourself and your business to new heights of prosperity. You'll find you get more and better qualified customers with greater ease than you thought possible.

I hope you enjoy what I've written and find it to be of some value. If you would like to send me a note about this book, feel free to write me at rich@thewritingking.com. If you enjoyed the book, please write a positive review.

What is Networking?

"Networking in business is the process of creating and maintaining mutually beneficial relationships with other business people." – Mark O'Donnell, President of RGA Networks

It is difficult for one person to succeed without the help of others. At the very least, a business needs clients in order to sell its products and services. Additionally, most also require vendors or suppliers of one sort or another, and many need contractors or advisors to help from time to time.

Thus, at its most basic level, networking means a business reaches out to find clients, vendors, suppliers, consultants, and others. As it grows, however, a business may also need new employees, to gather information about competitors and possible allies, and even buy or merge with other companies.

Let's look at a simple example: you are thinking about repainting your house. You've never done this before, and you would like to find somebody you can trust to get the job done.

You're cautious because you've heard horror stories from others about hiring contractors out of the phone book that resulted in substandard work, chipped paint, and colors that didn't match. In fact, one of your friends told you his house had been infected with termites because the painting job was so poor that bare wood was exposed to the elements, allowing the insects to get in and establish colonies.

What is Networking?

With this in mind, you want to make sure to get someone reputable to do the job. You know your friend Bill has many contacts in the business world, so you ask him, "I'm thinking of repainting my house, Bill. Do you know of any reputable painters?"

It's an interesting fact of human nature that people like to help others, especially those they know, like and trust. Thus, when you ask for help, assuming you are not abusing the privilege, it's very rare that you'll be turned down. That's one of the fundamental building blocks of networking – people want to help.

Bill may not personally know of any painters to recommend, but he will reach out to his network of business contacts to find out if they know of anybody who can help.

Chances are, since Bill is an excellent networker, he will get the name and contact information of a reputable house painter from one of his connections, let's say from Sam. From there, an introduction can be arranged, and since that painter had been recommended by somebody trusted, there is a much higher likelihood that you will be happy with the results.

If anything goes wrong, Bill will go back to back to the person who recommended the painter, in this example Sam, and say, "Hey, your friend didn't do this, this, and this."

Now Sam would go back to the painter, and say, "Look, they're not happy with the job." Hopefully the way humans work, that guy will want to make you happy, and so will fix it up so it won't become an issue.

As you can see from this example, business networking is about creating relationships with others, who are also building and maintaining relationships with other people.

This results in two advantages:

- You build up a circle of relationships with people that you can help and can also help you. It is vital to the concept of networking that relationships operate both ways.
- Because the people in your circle of relationships are also networking with other people, they can reach out and ask their network for help when needed. This dramatically increases your possibilities of getting things done.

In virtually every city in the United States, and probably much of the world, groups have been formed to support those who want to network with other business people. These groups generally have a yearly membership fee, and provide several services in addition to hosting regular networking meetings.

The Chamber of Commerce is a business federation which represents companies, businesses, and state and local chambers throughout the US and abroad. There is a chapter in virtually every city in the United States, and by joining you can reap the benefits of networking directly with businesses in your local area.

BNI (Business Networking International) is one of the largest networking groups in the United States. Only one person per profession specialty can join a chapter of BNI to eliminate competition among members.

https://www.bni.com/

Smaller regional groups such as RGA network (Revenue Generating Activities) provide excellent networking opportunities and usually have a more relaxed atmosphere and set of rules than larger organizations.

http://www.rganetwork.net

Rotary is a network of over a million people who work to help their communities. You'll find many interesting and powerful people as members.

http://rotary.org

Kiwanis is another service-oriented group designed to work with local communities and help when needed.

http://www.kiwanis.org/

Meetup.com offers many opportunities for networking for both business, and personal requirements. You can sign up on Meetup.com and search for groups of people who get together for just about any purpose. For example, to help with my writing career, I use Meetup to find writing-related groups within driving distance so that I can network with other authors.

http://meetup.com

In the world of virtual networking (also known as social media), you can be networking heavily with people and companies from all over the world. Sites such as LinkedIn, Facebook and, to a lesser extent, Twitter make this straightforward.

On these and other sites, online networking can be extremely powerful in today's world of fast communications, virtual conferencing, Webcams, and discussion forums.

Specialty networking groups, such as the Alliance of Independent Authors (for writers), serve to support the networking of people in specific professions. You can find these kinds of groups for virtually every field and profession that exists.

Outside of these formal networking groups, you can use tradeshows, conferences, classes, schools, and just about anywhere else where business people get together to build and maintain your network.

Of course, as you go about your daily activities in your career, you should be meeting like-minded business people and building relationships with them as well. This can include your peers in other companies, other people within your own company, vendors, suppliers, recruiters, consultants, and anyone else who could potentially be of value to you.

Networking done correctly can increase your ability to get things done by many times. The capacity to reach out to people that you know, like and trust to get help, advice, products, or services when you need them is invaluable for career growth and success.

What is Networking?

However, using networking incorrectly is at best a waste of time and at worse can cause harm to your reputation, career, and future. Just as you can be known, liked and trusted, your actions can also cause you to be known, disliked, and un-trusted.

That's why the underlying basic concept of business networking is **integrity**. Without integrity, networking is counterproductive and a waste of everyone's time.

Recap

- Successfully building and maintaining a network of like-minded professionals will expand your business.
- Incorrectly using networking can harm your business, reputation and income.
- Professional associations are an excellent way to network for your career growth.
- Networking groups such as the Chamber of Commerce, BNI, or RGA Network provide excellent sources of business contacts.
- You can network by physically attending networking meeting and by joining online groups.
- The foundation of networking is integrity.

Exercise

Use your favorite search engine to find local and online networking groups. Read the mission statement of several of these groups – usually you can find them either on their own page or on the About page of the site. Do any of these groups interest you? Decide if you want to visit them or check them out further online.

It's About Relationships

"At its most basic level, networking is connecting with like-minded, positive thinking individuals to share their contact and referral databases." – Mark O'Donnell, President of RGA Networks

In years past my job was to support the computer systems that served all the needs of a multi-billion-dollar company. This responsibility required getting to know many individuals who understood not just the technology, but the administration and concepts required to succeed.

Early in my career, I tended to fend for myself for the most part and hired or contacted others when I needed their skills or knowledge. I didn't expend any efforts in building any kind of relationships with these people, which meant that in their minds I was "just a client" and was treated the same as any other customer.

Thus, each time I reached out for help or advice, I had to introduce myself, make known what I needed, negotiate, sign the appropriate agreements, and then wait in line with everyone else. That worked fine for the most part in nonemergency or non-critical situations where it was time to go through the process.

However, over time I learned that this approach broke down rapidly where the need was more urgent. Since there was no relationship with those individuals and businesses, they had no incentive, other than financial, to go out of their way to provide what was needed.

It's About Relationships

My boss had an entirely different method of operation. He had meetings with many different people, sometimes in person and sometimes over the phone, who he'd met over the years. In fact, it seemed to me, at the time, that he was wasting large amounts of time in meaningless conversations.

He invited me to lunch with one of these business associates, and I found it interesting that it was more like a social event than a business meeting. They talked about the weather, sports, what was going on in each of their businesses, and other things in general, but there was no discussion of contracts, pending projects, or anything else of what I thought of as important.

For quite a while, I thought it was just one of his idiosyncrasies, something that he did that didn't make any sense to me. You know, everybody has quirks or behaviors that don't appear to be entirely rational but are harmless.

A few days after that meeting, we had some serious problems with one of our major computer systems. These lasted for days – I had exhausted every contingency plan, and had reached out to all the vendors in my Rolodex without coming up with a solution.

The boss finally intervened and called me over to his desk. He got on the phone with his friend from that lunch and had a conversation. He explained our problem and the friend replied that he couldn't help but he knew someone who could. Within a few hours, I had a team of specialists at my beck and call who resolved the issue quickly and efficiently.

I realized the important fact that I had been missing.

It's all about relationships.

Over the next few years, I began forming relationships with others in the industry, regardless of whether I needed their help at the time. I went to training meetings and introduced myself to everyone that I could find, and remained in contact with those people in the years that followed.

Everywhere I went, I worked to meet people, and when appropriate, build up a relationship with them, and keep that relationship going. This was not an easy time for an introverted shy person like me.

Five years later, we had a major system crash, the kind that causes computer people to have nightmares. The fact is that our computers were inoperable could potentially cost millions of dollars a day.

Within a matter of hours, after realizing that this was far beyond anything that the in-house staff could manage, I reached out to the people that I had built relationships with over the years, explaining the situation and asking them for help.

The crash had occurred late Friday evening, well outside of normal business hours. I had driven into the office to see what I could do, then, after calling my boss so he was informed, pulled out my Rolodex and started making phone calls to the network that had I built up over the past few years.

When my boss arrived at work a few hours later, he was surprised to find that I had a dozen specialists in the office

It's About Relationships

busy on the problem, as well as several other non-technical people to help where they could.

I remember the look on his face as two technicians set up temporary workstations so the people I brought in could work, and engineers were busy in the computer room lifting floor tiles to check cables and equipment.

He was even more surprised when he asked what all this was going to cost, and the owner of one of the companies replied, "You don't worry about cost when your neighbor's house is burning down. You put out the fire."

Over a dozen people gave up their weekend because I asked them to come in and help.

That's the power of networking.

Recap

- The purpose of networking is to establish and maintain long-term business relationships.
- By taking the time to get to know people, and to let them know you, they are much more likely to be there when you need them or to purchase your products and services over the long-term.
- Without establishing a networking relationship, you become just another client, vendor or consultant and will be treated as such.

Exercise

Pick a dozen people from your contact list. Send half of them an email reintroducing yourself and call the other half on the phone. For each one, bring up, if you remember, something interesting that you know about them. Add communicating with your network to your daily (or at least weekly) task list. Keep notes on the people in your contact list about hobbies, interests, and skillsets. Reviewing this before speaking with them will make your conversations more meaningful to them and advantageous to you over time.

Know, Like and Trust

"To be successful, you have to be able to relate to people; they have to be satisfied with your personality to be able to do business with you and to build a relationship with mutual trust." – George Ross

The last time you received a cold call from a salesman asking you to buy something, how motivated were you to make a purchase? In fact, did you even want to continue the conversation at all, or did you make efforts to terminate it as soon as possible?

When you cold-call someone, you're facing a basic problem: they don't know who you are, have no reason to trust you, and hence automatically don't like or are at best neutral about you.

Of course, cold-calling has its place in sales, it's just not terribly effective. Add to that the factor that most people who make these kinds of calls are not interested in forming a relationship at all – they're interested in making a sale.

Networking has an entirely different purpose – to form relationships which may or may not lead to business down the road.

In my role as Director of Technical Services and Computer Operations, I had authority to spend several million dollars a year, which made me very popular with many large computer resellers. Sometimes it seemed that not a day would go by where some salesman wanted to talk to me about replacing all our computer systems with their brand, or about selling me some newfangled product that would save vast sums of time and money.

In most cases, I didn't know the person who was calling or emailing me out of the blue, and because of that they didn't get very far. Usually these calls started out with a very brief introduction and quickly moved to the main point – could they talk to me about purchasing their product or service?

On the other hand, some vendors took a different approach. For example, Jimmy, one of my peers (the Director of Network Operations), introduced me to Tim, a senior salesperson from a major computer reseller. Jimmy spent a few minutes explaining that Tim could be trusted to do the right thing even if it didn't mean making a sale. I immediately made a lunch appointment to talk to Tim a week later.

This illustrates one of the significant approaches to networking – get someone trusted to make an introduction. In this case, since I trusted Jimmy, and trusted his judgment, I implicitly trusted Tim.

Tim arrived precisely on time, which is an important point when you're establishing a networking relationship, gave me a firm handshake, made good eye contact, and introduced me to Rusty, one of his engineers.

Always be on time for any networking appointments – in fact arrive slightly early if possible. This not only reinforces trust, but it gives you time in case there's traffic or any other unexpected delays.

The three of us went out to lunch together, and had a two hour long fruitful discussion about the computer industry, new trends in technology, and our respective hobbies, likes, and dislikes. The discussion moved to some of the problems that my department was experiencing and about running our computer systems. Tim made copious notes without volunteering to sell anything to resolve those problems.

We'll go over this in more detail later, but networking is not sales. In fact, they are completely different from each other. Networking is about listening and understanding, discussing and creating a relationship. Networking can lead to sales, but it's a longer-term approach.

Later, I put out a request for proposal to several hardware vendors for new computer systems, and Tim was included on the list. After several meetings to discuss our needs, he declined to bid because, "He felt that he couldn't provide the best ROI on the project." Instead, he recommended a different hardware vendor, who he believed could provide us the best solution.

Trust is vital asset in any networking relationship. Sometimes it's necessary to do the right thing and pass up on the short-term sale. Relationships take time and effort to create and maintain, yet dishonesty, even over a small thing, can cause irreparable damage.

At that moment, Tim gained my respect, and he became the preferential, and sometimes the only, bidder for any equipment purchases.

Know, Like and Trust

Other vendors came and went, but Tim remained high on my short list of vendors because I knew him as a person, liked him because of his ethics and abilities, and trusted him because I knew that he would do the right thing instead of doing what made him the most money.

The most important concept in networking is *know, like and trust*. Your objective when you meet people, speak to them, attend their meetings, give speeches, and everything else is to get them to know, like and trust you.

Think about it. Do you buy things from people that you don't know? If you don't like them, do you still purchase something from them? If you don't trust somebody, would you hand over your money?

When you network, you're laying the foundation for a relationship with one or more people.

Networking is for the long-term, not for a short-term sale or gain.

Recap

- The best way to establish a business relationship is to get someone who is known and trusted to set up an introduction.
- Being on time establishes trust. If you can't be trusted to respect someone's time, can you be trusted at all?
- Always greet people with a firm handshake and good eye contact. This puts the relationship on an even footing.
- The goal is to be known, liked and trusted.

Exercise

Pick one of your local contacts and take them to lunch. Talk to them, learn about their likes and dislikes, and keep the conversation away from sales and problems. Did the relationship improve?

Networking Is Not Sales

"Networking is marketing. Marketing yourself, marketing your uniqueness, marketing what you stand for." – Christine Comaford-Lynch

When you're networking, one of the biggest mistakes that you can make is to try to sell things to people. I know that sounds counterintuitive because, obviously, when you get right down to it, the reason most people network is because they want to sell something.

Joe is attending a network meeting because he wants to sell his herbal supplements.

Sally, standing next to him, is trying to sell real estate and get people interested in buying the homes that she has for sale.

At a computer convention, Jim is working the crowd because he's trying to find a new job, and he wants to get some contacts in the industry willing to make him an offer.

And Debbie is trying to sell her new book, so she's constantly posting on Facebook, Goodreads, Google Plus, and everywhere else she could find, asking, demanding, and begging people to buy it from her.

It shouldn't come as any big surprise that all four of these people don't achieve the results they desire through their networking efforts. In fact, all of them declared that they felt that networking was a waste of time.

Networking Is Not Sales

The problem these four confronted had nothing to do with networking.

For networking to be effective, you must understand that it is not a sales tool. In fact, it is highly unlikely that you will be able to sell anything while you are networking.

In a networking meeting, you are not going to sell your vitamin supplements, your real estate, your books, your computer consulting services, or anything else.

What you will be able to do, if you network correctly, is build relationships with the people whom you network with, and that will result in sales over the longer term – but only a few of those sales will be from the actual people in the group.

If you went to a networking meeting, stood up, and asked to see a show of hands of how many people in the room wanted to sell something, most likely everyone would raise their hand.

On the other hand, if you asked how many people are there to buy something, you would find very few people, if any, saying that that is the reason why they are networking. Clearly there's a disconnection which is caused by a basic misunderstanding of the purpose of networking.

You are not engaged in networking to sell.

You're not engaged in networking to buy either.

Your purpose in attending networking groups, joining the Chamber of Commerce, taking part in activities from associations related to your profession, and mingling with people in conventions, is to build relationships.

When you're meeting with someone, get them to talk by asking questions about their hobbies, their likes, what sports they appreciate, and so forth. Keep the subject away from anything controversial such as politics and religion, and avoid negativity.

Your objective is to get them to tell you about themselves. By asking questions and then listening to the answers, you build up a picture of your networking friend, and find out how you can help them.

Of course, the conversation shouldn't be one way. Offer similar information about yourself, your hobbies, your likes, favorite sports, and any other noncontroversial subject. This keeps the conversation flowing back and forth so that it is balanced and you both learn about each other. Most of the time, when you show an interest in someone, it is natural for them to ask you about yourself, but if you make it about them for the better part of the conversation, they will believe you to be a brilliant conversationalist.

Use your networking meetings to inform others about what you can do, and what kind of skills and people you're looking for. Tell them about yourself, your business, as well as your needs and desires.

At the same time, listen to what they have to say about their business and what they need as well.

Networking Is Not Sales

By doing this, they begin to know who you are; they will like you because you're listening to them, and they will begin to trust you because you are showing them respect and you're interested in who they are and what they have to say.

To make networking effective, you must change your MO.

Part of the problem is networking organizations often portray themselves in a manner that makes them appear to be sales-related. They promote that you can come to a meeting and tell people about your products and services, and they may even go so far as to say you'll find people interested in purchasing what you've got.

You'll have to ignore all of that.

If you were having dinner with a friend, would you try and sell them a new car, real estate, or consulting services? More than likely, if you did so they would either politely change the subject to something else, or become upset with you. After all, it's supposed to be a friendly dinner, not a sales meeting.

This doesn't mean you don't talk about business or mention your products or services. It just means you treat it more as a friendly discussion than as a sales call.

That way, when you're in a conversation with someone else, and they mention that they need a service or product, you'll be able to refer someone in your network to them to help them out. This is because you listened when they told you about their skills, knowledge and abilities.

And the other people in your network will do the same thing for you.

That's how you take advantage of networking. Communicate with the other people in your network on a regular basis so that you understand their business, needs and wants, and so that they understand the same from you.

If you do this regularly, without trying to sell, you'll find that you'll start getting referrals from others to your own business. You'll also find that you will be giving referrals to other people in your network.

Over time, this will result in a dramatic increase in the amount of business that you receive. The best thing about it is, because you're getting referrals from people who need and want your service or product, they are far more likely to purchase than with leads from advertising, cold-calling or any other form of promotion.

Recap

- Networking consists of communicating with like-minded people in or related to your profession.
- To get the maximum value from your network, avoid sales-related discussions.
- Sales and leads will come to you indirectly as your network grows and gets stronger.
- Leads from networking will be far more qualified than any of those gained from other sources.

Exercise

Meet with a member of your network and try to sell your products and services to them. Afterwards, meet with someone else and have a friendly discussion to find out more about them and their business. Which of these discussions was more fruitful?

How Can I Help?

"Always give without remembering and receive without forgetting." – William Barkley

I drove over 100 miles to get to the job interview in Camarillo. That was a long way to drive based upon a five-minute phone interview with Alasdair, the software manager of BIF AccuTell, a company that manufactured hardware to allow water districts to monitor and control water systems.

Just a few days before, I decided to look for another job, and now had over a dozen interviews lined up, including one all the away up in Seattle. It was a busy time, but I was determined to find a new position elsewhere as fast as possible.

Even though my job as Vice President of Consulting kept me extraordinarily busy, I maintained a sizable network of contacts from conventions, training courses, and exhibit floors.

For years, I kept in touch with these people via email, in person, and on the phone. The idea was just to remain in contact with them, find out how they're doing, and asking them if there was anything I could do to help them out.

Usually they didn't need anything, but occasionally someone would reply that they were looking for a consultant with a certain skill, a new employee, some technical documentation, and occasionally even a reference for a job.

How Can I Help?

Wherever possible, I gave them what help they needed without asking for anything in return. Sometimes I could help them directly, but more often I passed along a reference to somebody who could give them what they needed.

For example, one day I got a call asking for help. Their computer had crashed, and the data was destroyed. If they couldn't restore that information, they would basically be out of business.

I sent over a technician right away, and he recovered their information by the end of the day. To them it was magic, although we did that kind of thing all the time.

Thus, when I decided to move on and find a job somewhere else, the first thing I did was open my Rolodex and start contacting people in my network.

I was amazed at the response – no one had any positions available, but they each gave me the names of other companies that might be able to help.

When you're looking for a job, taking the traditional route of sending in your resume, and hoping that it gets picked among the thousands that they receive, can take an immense amount of time and effort. If you've ever been job hunting, you know what I'm talking about.

The advantage of using a network to hunt for a job is that you go through the back door, so to speak, either to the right person to make a hiring decision, or to someone who can introduce you to that person.

I managed to line up a dozen interviews in an amazingly short time because each of those managers received a personal reference about me from someone they trusted – someone in my network.

Most people enjoy being helped. After all, life is tough and there are many obstacles to success. In the world of business, some of the major barriers are skills, time, and knowledge, and if you can provide those, you will become highly respected and sought after.

The fastest and most effective way to build a strong network is to communicate regularly, to offer help, and to follow through by either personally helping or to provide a reference to someone who can.

The old saying that "it is better to give than to receive" doubly applies to networking. Help and giving builds the foundation and solidifies the bonds between you and the people in your network.

Anyone can talk, and everyone is always asking for, or demanding things, but the most powerful people, the ones who can be trusted and who are competent, help others and give on a regular basis.

Helping other people, which builds up your credibility, causes them to like and trust you, and you'll find your network to be very responsive on those occasions when you reach out to them for help.

How Can I Help?

Being willing to help and give, as opposed to asking and demanding help, is the glue that puts your network into overdrive.

Conversely, continually asking for things, demanding help, and selling is a great way to sabotage your ability to network with others.

That long drive to Camarillo, and all the networking behind it, paid off. A few days after the interview, Alastair offered me a job as a Senior Designer, which I accepted. Additionally, I was offered a second job as Vice President of Consulting in North Long Beach on the weekends (part-time) for a small startup company which I also accepted.

The true power of networking is giving and offering help to others.

Recap

- While expanding your network, give freely without keeping a ledger.
- Being a giver will strengthen the bonds with people in your network so they will be willing to help when you reach out to them.

Exercise

Call up a few of your contacts and have a conversation with them. Sometime during the conversation in a sincere manner, ask them if they need anything. Most likely they will thank you and decline. Let them know that if they need anything they should email or call you at any time. After you've done this for half a dozen contacts, did you notice any change in the way they communicated?

A good question I see asked a lot among professional business people is, "What do you need next?" When you ask the question, be prepared to listen and help them make connections as they need them. This question puts you in the position of being the person offering help and assistance; a very powerful place to come from.

It's Not About You

"You can make more friends in two months by becoming interested in other people, than you can in two years by trying to get other people interested in you." – Dale Carnegie

Several years ago, I managed twelve technical people, mostly application coders and designers. Dave worked for me and was the Senior Designer and coder on a critical application product for one of our top clients.

Dave and I went to a computer convention together, flying all the way from Los Angeles to Las Vegas to attend. I learned a lot from those four days, although the knowledge I gained had nothing to do with computers, technology, or anything like that.

The two of us wandered around the convention floor between sessions (1 to 2 hour long talks by experts) and networked with anybody we could find. Each day we spent a couple of hours in the exhibit hall, wandering around the booths, shaking hands, and talking to vendors, customers, and attendees to try and build up our network.

The first day after we arrived, we hit the convention floor and I spotted Daphne, who was the Development Manager at another consulting company. I walked over to her, shook hands, and introduced her to Dave.

Dave spent the next fifteen minutes telling her all about himself, beginning with how great he was, then listed out some of the larger projects he'd been on, and finished with a glowing report about his abilities.

Poor Daphne barely got a word in edgewise, and she kept looking over to me as if I was supposed to come to her rescue. Finally, I took mercy on her, told Dave we had to move on, and the two of us continued to the rest of the booths in the exhibit hall.

At first I was amused as I observed Dave tell everyone all about himself. After a while, it got tiring, so I wandered off so I could do some serious networking.

My approach was quite different. At one of the booths, for example, I talked with a technical person named Seymour who was manning the booth of one of our vendors. Engaging him into a conversation, I found out several things about his life, his job, how much he made, and what he hoped to accomplish at the convention. I finished the conversation by handing him my card, letting them know that if he needed anything he should give me a call.

I repeated the same approach to over a hundred people during the four-day convention. I took each person's business card, asked them about themselves, and wrote a few notes on the back so I could remember who they were later. When I returned to the office, I made it a point to send an email to every useful contact, thanking them for their time and repeating something that I'd learned from them talking about themselves.

The business card of those contacts that I determined to be of little to no value got thrown in the trash. No sense cluttering my contact list with people that I had no intention of ever communicating with again.

To my knowledge, Dave never heard back from any of the people that he contacted at the convention hall. On the other hand, I talked to many of them afterwards, and went to great lengths to stay in contact by making a phone call or sending an email at least every few months.

In fact, two weeks after the convention, Seymour called me because he'd been looking for a technical manual which was currently out of print. He remembered our conversation, and wondered if I had a copy that he could borrow. I had one in the mail to him the next day, and we have remained in contact ever since.

A few years later, when I needed to find a job quickly, I reached out to Seymour and he gave me several great references, one of which granted me an interview.

It's important to understand that while you are networking, the conversation should not center around you. Your mission, while you're talking to the other person, is to find out about them, and plant seeds they will remember later.

By doing this, you practically guarantee that your business card won't just be thrown in a drawer – instead, you'll probably get an invitation on LinkedIn to join them in their professional network (if you don't take the lead and do that step yourself.)

On the other hand, focusing the conversation on yourself, your abilities, your needs, your products, and what you want to sell, makes it very likely that your business card will be carefully filed in the trashcan next to the desk.

Recap

- People like to talk about themselves, especially if they believe you're intent on hearing about them. Make it clear that you're interested in what they have to say.
- Always tell them to contact you if they need something.
- Keep notes of your conversation so that when you talk to them later you can mention what you have already talked about. This is a great way to impress someone – it shows that you were listening.
- If the contact is worth maintaining, enter their information in your contact database or, better yet, connect to them on LinkedIn.
- On the other hand, if the contact is not useful or even counterproductive then throw the business card away and don't waste your time on them.

Exercise

The next few times you network with someone, take the time to ask them about themselves, and refrain from monopolizing the conversation with information about you. What were the results?

Act Professional

"Believe passionately in what you do, and never knowingly compromise your standards and values. Act like a true professional, aiming for true excellence, and the money will follow." – David Maister

One of the most important reasons to network is to build your reputation among your peers, clients, vendors, and others related to your industry or locality. Don't let your appearance and demeanor undermine what you're trying to achieve.

Steve was my first manager and mentor, and he was one of the best networkers that I've ever known. He had a technical background, but unlike most computer people, was very outgoing and networking came naturally to him.

Watching him in action was a joy to behold, and he exuded confidence and professionalism, which was precisely what our young startup company needed.

When Steve walked into a room to meet someone, he stretched out his hand and gave a firm handshake, at the same time making good eye contact. He always had a friendly smile on his face, regardless of how he felt, and didn't wait for the other person to open the conversation. Instead, he asked them how they were or how their business was doing.

Regardless of how the conversation went, he kept it under control, either flowing with the subject or cleanly switching to a different topic if necessary. He was equally comfortable talking about the weather or negotiating contracts with difficult and demanding clients.

During a particularly hostile encounter with a client, Steve maintained firm control of the situation. He didn't get angry (during the meeting), kept a smile on his face, and expertly handled the discussion to a good conclusion. One of his philosophies was that emotions such as anger or annoyance have no place in business.

He taught me that professionals dress appropriate to the image they are attempting to portray. On occasion, he wore formal attire because that was expected when negotiating a large contract with a big client. In other instances, when he was playing the part of a computer specialist, he'd wear casual jeans and a t-shirt.

He stressed that it was important to be well groomed and to never wear colognes or perfumes when meeting with clients or others. Sometimes people have allergies or they may be turned off by strong scents, but no one ever got upset by the lack of a smell.

Another important lesson he taught is to always be prepared with paper for note-taking, at least two pens (one for him and one for the client if necessary), business cards and copies of promotional materials.

Steve was my manager for four years before he moved on to a different company. The last time we talked, he was a Vice President at Walt Disney Studios, and was busy mingling with the crowd at a computer networking convention.

I have no doubt that he attained that position because he understood how to network to make the contacts that he needed to succeed.

Recap

- When you are networking, be confident and sure of yourself.
- Be prepared with paper, at least two pens, and business cards.
- Dress to fit the image that you want to portray, and be well groomed.
- Don't wear any perfumes or colognes when networking.
- Greet people confidently by shaking their hand firmly and making good eye contact without challenging them.
- Smile.
- Keep your emotions at home or in the car. They have no role when you are networking.

Exercise

Examine yourself and your demeanor objectively. Can you change your dress, your appearance, or the way you meet or deal with others to be more effective? Start with something small, like giving firm handshakes; do it until it becomes a habit (a couple of weeks), then find another area to address.

The Networking Meeting

"Networking is an essential part of building wealth." –
Armstrong Williams

Some networking organizations put on what are basically
mixers, where they invite several hundred people to a hotel,
restaurant or some other large venue. They provide light
snacks and drinks, and the event lasts for several hours.

The purpose of these mixers is to exchange business cards,
make introductions, and mill around talking to people about
their organizations, skills, talents, and profession. These can
be very useful to certain professionals such as lawyers and
realtors who need to find clients quickly.

These types of networking meetings are usually attended by
a very large number of people, several hundred or more,
jammed into the venue. For those who are introverted, that
many people packed into a room can be a daunting and
frustrating experience.

Alternately, several organizations sponsor regular and
structured networking meetings available to any person that
wants to form a relationship with like-minded people and
businesses. Your local Chamber of Commerce, BNI, and
RGA network, among others, all run weekly meetings in
various locations in cities all over the country.

To join these groups and take advantage of all their services,
you'll need to pay a yearly fee. This can range anywhere from

The Networking Meeting

$100 all the way up to a thousand or more, depending on the group.

Most of them host meetings that occur once a week, often at local restaurants during breakfast, lunch, or dinner hours. This allows business people to attend the meeting without losing productive time from their normal work hours.

It's important be punctual and arrive on time if you want to get the full benefit of the meeting. Some groups impose penalties on those who come in late.

As soon as you arrive at one of these meetings, you'll generally be greeted by someone who shakes your hand and makes you feel welcome in the group. After that, you find a seat, sit down, optionally order food from the restaurant, and talk to the people around you.

Because these meetings are intended to be done between work hours for busy professionals, they usually start and finish on time, and are run on a tight agenda.

After some opening statements by the meeting director or leader, everyone in the room will give a thirty-second introduction (elevator speech), quickly describing who they are, what kind of referrals they're looking for, and a few words about their business. It's important to keep introductions brief and to the point so that everyone gets a chance to talk.

Take the time to craft this speech and practice it, preferably in front of a mirror. This should roll off of your tongue without you having to think about it. It should be short enough and concise enough to give others a reason to ask questions, or as P.T. Barnum said, "Always leave them wanting more."

Once the introductions are out of the way, one member gets to give a speech lasting 10 or 15 minutes, and following that there may be another 10-minute activity. Finally, the meeting closes with announcements of any special events or other meetings in the area.

If all you do is attend the meetings and nothing else, you won't receive the full value of attendance. To increase the value, set up separate meetings outside of the meeting to talk with individuals one-on-one.

These additional meetings can be scheduled for any time convenient to those in attendance. The idea is for two, and sometimes more, people to get to know one another.

Do not use these to attempt to sell your products or services. That's not the purpose and if you do that, then you more than likely will drive people away from you.

Instead, when you meet one-on-one with someone, ask them about themselves. Pick some innocent topics such as the recent weather, a local sport, hobbies, and so forth, and talk to them about it.

Keep the conversation light and away from controversial subjects such as politics. Your objective is not to get into a debate; it is to build bonds with like-minded professionals.

Take notes, and be sure to record those notes in your contact database so you can refer to them later.

The Networking Meeting

Get their business card, and jot down something memorable on it so that later, when you're entering it into your contact list or connecting with them on LinkedIn, you can jog your memory.

Finally, enjoy yourself at these meetings and at the meetings after meetings. The more you relax and enjoy yourself, the more other people will loosen up. This makes them more willing to talk to you, and makes you more interesting as a contact.

Recap

- One type of networking meeting gets a group of people together to exchange contact information. These tend to be unstructured and can be daunting to introverted people.
- Networking groups such as the Chamber of Commerce, BNI, and RGA networks put on regular – usually weekly – meetings in your local area, that are very structured.
- These meetings charge a yearly fee, so if you join, make sure you take advantage of all the opportunities they give you.
- Keep your elevator speech to the time limit allowed for in the meeting. If you talk too long, most people will tune you out anyway.
- Many of these meetings allow members to schedule speeches. Take advantage of these to let everyone know about you and your business.
- One-on-one discussions outside of these meetings help to get to know someone. It is in these meetings that relationships are formed.
- Remember that meetings outside of meetings are intended to build relationships; not to make sales.
- Most of all, loosen up and enjoy yourself.

Exercise

Attend a local networking meeting as a guest and observe the proceedings carefully. Is the meeting held at a location with affordable food? Is the venue clean, does it have good parking, and is it well attended? Do the members appear to be happy and getting value from the meeting? Decide – do you want to join or continue looking for other networking groups?

If you do decide to continue to attend, make a point of sitting with a different group every time to maximize the number of people you can meet.

Oftentimes these groups host additional events or do charitable work. If you want to become known as a "team player", offer to volunteer your services and/or any resources you may have that could be helpful.

Social Media

"Social media is changing the way we communicate and the way we are perceived, both positively and negatively. Every time you post a photo, or update your status, you are contributing to your own digital footprint and personal brand."
– Amy Jo Martin

These days, it is vital to take advantage of social media to improve your ability to network locally, regionally, nationally, and even worldwide.

The truth of the matter is that if you don't maintain a good presence online, you are passing up on a substantial source of leads and income.

The most significant social media platforms include Facebook, LinkedIn, and Twitter. At the very least, make sure you have a presence on these three sites; this includes setting up a profile or page, keeping it up-to-date, and posting relevant content. Additionally, on LinkedIn and Facebook, you should join groups and like pages which have topics related to your business, customers, suppliers, or interests.

- **LinkedIn** - For professional networking, LinkedIn is far and away the most important social media platform. My book, *Focus on LinkedIn*, goes into detail about how to set up and use this network.
- **Facebook** - On Facebook, don't use your personal account for business networking. Instead, create a page specifically for your business. Keep that page up-

to-date with information about your company, and be sure to link it to your LinkedIn profile.

- **Twitter** - Every business needs to have a Twitter account, and use it to communicate information about their business. Post news and information about your business to your Twitter feed.
- **YouTube** – This is the largest, most active social network of them all. It's owned and operated by Google. So, by adding videos regularly and ensuring each one links back to your sites, blogs, and social media profiles, you tend to attract Google, and other search engines, and thus get more traffic.

For all four of these platforms, ensure you have consistent branding which includes a logo, graphics banner, and description. To avoid confusion in your marketplace, it is essential that your brand looks the same across all platforms.

To build a network on each, it is important to take the time on a regular basis to do the work necessary to engage with people on both a group level and a one-on-one basis.

Think of networking on the Internet in the same way that you think of it in the physical world.

- Make sure your profiles and pages are set up correctly, reflect your brand, and look professional. Just as in a real store or business, people won't come in if your locale looks unkempt and messy.
- When someone visits, take the time to shake their hand, introduce yourself, ask them how they are, and get into a conversation with them. This happens when

they leave a message on your page, reply to one of your comments in a group, or otherwise communicate.

- Spend the time to find the pages and groups of others in related fields and join or like them. By doing this, you are showing your support for those other people.
- Contribute to conversations on groups and pages by replying to comments and posting questions or statements of your own. This will build up your credibility and reputation.

Treat your social media accounts in the same way that you think of a physical networking meeting, tradeshow, exhibit hall, or other place where people search each other out.

Once someone takes the time to answer your question in a group, leave a comment on your page or respond in some other way; take the time to open a conversation with them. Follow the same procedure that you would if you met them at a networking or other event.

I make it a point to spend 30 to 60 minutes each day on social media. This includes LinkedIn, Facebook, Twitter, and Goodreads (a social media platform for readers and authors.)

What do I do during this time?

- On Facebook, quickly review the posts for the last day for about a dozen groups, respond to a few conversations, and post something from my websites in each one if applicable.
- On LinkedIn, respond to the status updates shown on my home page if applicable.

Social Media

- Like posts, graphics and videos that apply to my business and interests.
- Invite people to link my pages and join the Facebook groups that I run.
- Post an update on my Facebook wall and LinkedIn home page with something useful, such as a video (always from my blog) for other people to enjoy.
- On YouTube, like and subscribe to half a dozen videos, and leave a comment, if appropriate, on each one.

The first few days this routine took hours, but as I got the hang of it I found that in 30 minutes I could make a couple of dozen comments, like a dozen videos, and another dozen graphics, create 6 to 12 small posts of my own, and respond to any messages from individuals.

After a few weeks of this routine, I began getting qualified business leads, just as with any other networking activities.

Recap

- Create your profile on LinkedIn.
- Create a Facebook page for your business.
- Create a Twitter account.
- Ensure all your social media profiles portray your brand.
- Join groups and like pages related to your business and interests.
- Regularly update your social media.
- Post, like, and share things constantly.
- Engage in conversations in your groups and pages.

Exercise

If you don't have a Facebook page for your business, a LinkedIn profile, and a Twitter, create them all now (or the ones that are missing.) Set up the profiles to match your brand. Join groups and like pages that match your business and interests.

Virtual Networking

"If we all work together there is no telling how we can change the world through the impact of promoting positivity online." – Germany Kent

Once you've established your social media presence, look for groups of people on relevant social media platforms including Facebook, LinkedIn, Google Plus. Many people who can be helpful to your business will be happy to network with you.

When I first began my writing career, I was having difficulty finding resources such as book cover designers who would do quality work at prices that I could afford. I'd already paid for three covers at $500 each and was severely disappointed by the results.

I reached out to my online writing network, and received back several references for inexpensive cover designers, proofreaders, and editors working from overseas.

This enabled me to get high quality work done at significantly reduced prices. Some of the contractors I hired came from countries with a much lower cost of living, and thus they didn't need to charge as much for their work to make a decent wage.

Others were students who needed experience in their field, a few were starting new lines of business and wanted to build up their portfolio, and for one it was a hobby, and she just wanted to make a few extra dollars.

Virtual Networking

Virtual networking gives you more than just the ability to find inexpensive and skilled suppliers and contractors.

Networking online increases the pool of experts who are available on any subject, no matter how small. Billions of people are available on the Internet, many of them practically begging for contact and communications with other people. Over time, you can build an international network of people who will enrich you in so many more ways than just selling more books or products.

You have access to people of all ages, students, professionals, interns, beginners, and just about everything in between. All you need to do is find the right online groups, with the correct mixture of people to support you in your professional life.

Many platforms have built-in translation tools to make it easy to communicate with people of other nationalities who don't speak your language.

You can find online forums matching your profession with a few quick Google searches. Joining them is usually a matter of submitting your request and waiting for approval from an administrator. Many groups charge a fee, often yearly, to get the full advantage of their services. Others are free for the asking.

You can increase the power of your networking by taking part in online video or audio chats using tools such as Google Hangouts or Skype. These allow two or more people to communicate using Webcams on the computer, tablet, or smart phone. Since you can all see each other, you get the full range of communication including verbal, visual, and written.

Take advantage of virtual networking, when appropriate, to increase your network to worldwide levels. When you combine virtual networking with attending groups in your local area, you can truly push your business up to new levels of prosperity.

Just like networking in person, you get out of this what you put into it. Adding helpful comments, asking intelligent questions that invite discussion, being willing to stop and research the answer to someone else's question, even though you don't' know the answer yourself, are just a few ways you can become a respected contributor to the group, and it will allow you to reach out to individual members from a position of respect as a thought leader.

You must be careful to ration the time that you spend on your virtual networking activities. Interacting with others can become very addicting, and the disadvantage of online networking is that you can do it anytime from anywhere on your smartphone, laptop, tablet, or desktop computer. Because of this, it's quite possible to waste away hours every single day doing activities which have no value to your business.

Recap

- Virtual networking gives you access to people and resources across the entire planet.
- Due to differences in the cost of living in different localities, using virtual networking you can dramatically decrease the cost of getting work done.
- Technologies such as Google Hangouts and Skype give you the ability to engage in videoconferencing.
- Engaging with others in online forums is a great way to network and make new contacts in your industry.
- Ration the time that you spend online because it's quite easy to lose hours every single day.

Exercise

Find several associations or other networking groups that operate primarily online. Read through their website and determine if you believe these groups have value. Join if appropriate. Ask other people in your personal network to recommend worthwhile forums and mastermind groups.

Conclusion

"Nothing liberates your greatness like the desire to help, the desire to serve." – Marianne Williamson

The important point stressed over and over in this book is that networking is not a sales tool; rather, it is a way to build up your credibility and reputation among others in your locality, your profession, your suppliers, and your customers.

Thus, the set of skills needed to be successful are not the same as those you would use to make a sale or to market a product. In general, you won't be giving long presentations about your products or services and you won't be meeting with people in your network to sell them something.

Instead, you'll be talking to people about your life, your likes and dislikes, your favorite sports or hobbies, and subjects of a similar nature. You'll be listening to others talk about the weather, a local event, their hobbies or favorite sports, and other subjects that they want to discuss.

Of course, you'll also be discussing your profession and your business, but your purpose is to inform instead of trying to gain sales or buyers.

You should go into networking with a casual and lighthearted approach rather than being serious and formal about it. People respond to humor, good news, and well-planned, successful events. Everyone works long and hard all day long, so it's counterproductive to enforce seriousness or formality (other than scheduling) in your networking activities.

Conclusion

Your purpose in your network is to meet other people who can potentially be of benefit to you, your business, and your profession and get them to know, like and trust you so that they will refer their friends, clients, vendors, suppliers and business associates (and even complete strangers) to you and your business.

The concept of "know, like and trust" is one of the most important concepts of networking. For someone to refer you to their friends and business associates, they must:

- Know about you, your profession, and your business.
- Like you, which means they feel affinity toward you.
- And they must trust you because they'll be referring you to people who are important in their lives.

Networking can occur in person, at local networking meetings, conventions, trade shows, courses, schools, and just about anywhere people in your profession congregate.

You can also network online (virtual networking) by taking advantage of social media such as Facebook, Google Plus, LinkedIn, and other platforms. Tools such as Google Hangouts and Skype can be used for videoconferencing, which, when used properly, can be a very effective form of networking.

By taking advantage of both in-person and virtual networking, you can literally push your business to the limits of expansion. Technology today gives you the ability to communicate with people all over the planet as easily as talking to the person in the next room.

However, using networking inappropriately, such as mistaking it for a sales tool, will result in lowering your credibility, pushing people away, and harming your business.

Find groups, either online or locally, that consist of people who can aid your business and your profession and career. Generally, each group will charge a yearly fee, so make sure you join ones that are important and that you will use.

Most importantly, loosen up and relax and enjoy networking. Have fun and don't take it too seriously. Remember that networking takes time to grow, and if you put in the right amount of energy and effort, it will pay you back in a steady stream of highly qualified referrals.

Join the Business Networking for Profit group on Facebook to continue the discussion about networking.

http://smooth.li/group

Before you go

If you scroll to the last page in this eBook, you will have the opportunity to leave feedback and share the book with Before You Go. I'd be grateful if you turned to the last page and shared the book.

Also, if you have time, please leave a review. Positive reviews are incredibly useful. If you didn't like the book, please email me at rich@thewritingking.com and I'd be happy to receive your input.

linkedin.thewritingking.com

Bonus: Interview with Mark O'Donnell

Richard Lowe: I'm here with Mark O'Donnell, the President of RGA Networks, and I'm interviewing him on the purpose of networking, why people should network and the advantages of doing it.

Mark, thank you for coming.

Mark O'Donnell: Thank you for having me Richard; it's an honor to be interviewed by you.

Richard Lowe: Thank you. So, let's begin by talking about you and your background.

Mark O'Donnell: I'm Mark O'Donnell, President and founder of the networking organization called RGA Networks. A lot of people want to know what RGA Networks stands for because in the networking community and world, a lot of the organizations use lettered acronyms.

The letters RGA mean Revenue Generating Activity, because I believe, as salesperson and a business owner myself, that what you should be doing during business hours is activities that create revenue, or you should be doing tasks that become revenue-generating activities.

I have a broad-based work background. I moved to Florida in 2002 for two reasons. We wanted to move down while we were young enough and while we could enjoy Florida, and to get away from the Midwest cold.

Bonus: Interview with Mark O'Donnell

We moved to a beautiful coastal town called Dunedin, which is a beautiful place to visit. A year later we moved to Clearwater, where we have lived for the past eleven years.

I worked for over fifteen years for the National Museum of Transport in St Louis, Missouri. It's a transportation museum; they have one of the largest collections of antique automobiles, trains, and planes in the world.

After moving here, I took a couple of sales jobs, and realized the necessity of networking because of the ability to meet and connect with a large group of individuals who can help introduce future clients.

Richard Lowe: Explain to me what you mean by networking.

Mark O'Donnell: Networking is connecting with like-minded, positive thinking individuals, to share their contact and referral database.

For example, suppose my neighbor asked me, "My wife and I are thinking of repainting our house. Mark, do you know of any painters?"

I would say that I don't personally know of any but let me ask my network if they have anyone to refer. I would stand up in a room of the twenty or thirty attendees and ask, "Hey, my neighbors are looking to get their house painted. Who do you know?"

Networking is like a strong word of mouth referral. Because several things start happening when you make that request. One, a person who eats lunch with me — they're usually weekly meetings, often very regular meetings – is not going to give me the name of painters that they don't know, like and trust.

And then they're going to tell that painter that this is for their friend from their networking group. So, when I introduce them to my neighbor, he's going to more than likely get the job because it's a word of mouth referral, "Hey, Mark has recommended this guy to paint our house."

Someone in the group will usually come back with a referral, someone they know, like and trust. I'll pass that person's name over to my neighbors. Since it's a personal reference, they assume (rightly) that they can trust him.

If anything goes wrong, I'm going to then go back to the person who recommended the painter and say, "Hey, your friend didn't do this, this and this and the neighbors are not happy."

Hopefully the way humans work, that painter will want to keep his customer and the guy who referred him happy, that he will fix whatever was wrong and it won't become an issue.

Richard Lowe: You used a term "know, like and trust." Can you explain that a little more?

Mark O'Donnell: You need to know somebody and know that they have the talent that you seek for them to do your task. You wouldn't go to an auto mechanic to get your hair cut, nor would you go to the beauty salon to get your oil changed.

Bonus: Interview with Mark O'Donnell

So, you must know them, you need to know that they know the craft. A lot of time that comes with documentation: they've graduated from a university or trade school that has taught them the way to do what needs to be done. Sometimes it's based on experience or testimonials from others.

Following that, you must like someone to want to do business with them. It's a very strong factor; it's almost 90% of your decision. If you felt that you've had a bad experience at a big grocery store, you probably don't shop at that big grocery store as often as you would if you felt you liked the people there.

Finally, most importantly in the "know, like and trust" factor is the trust. The trust is where the money floats from your hand into the other person's hand, because you trusted that they changed your oil and put your car back in working order and you can now safely go travel the roads.

You trust that when the lady spins you around in the chair in the hair salon that you're not bald. You trust that the baker who baked your kid's birthday cake, that that cake's going to taste good and won't be filled with metal shavings.

If people know you and like you, but they don't trust you, they're not going to give you their money.

Richard Lowe: Can you give an example of that?

Mark O'Donnell: I needed to get my car detailed. I hired a guy and he did an okay job but he wasn't the world's best detailer for the price that I paid. I thought it should have been a very good job.

In conversations with other friends, they had had a similar experience. We just chalked it up to experience or lack of caring or something like that. I won't choose to spend my money with him again, because I've found a place that will detail my car to my specifications, and it's less expensive.

Thus, I didn't trust that guy to detail my car again because of how it turned out the last time. The sad thing for that guy is that he no longer gets my referrals when somebody says "Your car always looks so nice; how do you keep it that way?" Instead, I send him to the place that is less expensive and does a better job.

Richard Lowe: Do you have an example of one that worked well for you?

Mark O'Donnell: One referral that worked well for me would be you, for instance, Richard. My friend was looking to get their LinkedIn profile updated; I guess they were getting back into the job market.

I told you about it and you two connected. When I followed up with him I asked, "How is Richard doing?"

He said, "Oh my God, he's fantastic, he's really doing a great job",

I thought, "Good", so you're in my book when somebody needs a writer, a content writer, or LinkedIn information.

Richard Lowe: Well, thank you. You used another word there, "referral". Why don't you explain what that means?

Bonus: Interview with Mark O'Donnell

Mark O'Donnell: There's a lead and a referral. A lot of people get those two confused.

I tell people I send flowers when people are alive. I don't believe in sending flowers to funerals, because the people that you love and cherish that have passed on are already dead.

So, I like to send the flowers when they're alive. I look for a florist that thinks outside the box. When I ask for a referral – I like to use locally owned, small businesses – I say something like, "I have friends in Illinois; does anybody know a florist in central Illinois?"

Someone will answer, "Yeah, I know Jacqueline, a florist."

"Great, you know the owner. Do you have her cellphone?"

"Yeah, here's the number."

"Do you mind if you call her to tell her I'm going to be calling to order some flowers for my aunt who lives there?"

"Yes, I will."

That takes the referral a step further. Jacqueline is now aware that you have referred her to me, so you're going to be bringing her business. Jacqueline is going to take a whole lot better care of me than if I was just Joe Schmoe walking in off the street, because Jacqueline will now want to impress me and she'll want to impress the one who referred me to her.

When asked how that referral worked out with Jacqueline, I'll either say, "Oh my God, I loved her", or, "She was the worst florist in world, quit recommending her."

A lead is when you ask, "Does anybody know a florist?" and somebody goes on their phone, gets three names and numbers, and gives them to you.

Those are leads, there's no connection, there's no, "Hey, my friend Richard Lowe said I should call", they'd most likely answer, "Who?"

Richard Lowe: How do you start a conversation with someone you haven't met before?

Mark O'Donnell: First, you introduce yourself. Just walk up, shake their hand, look them in the eye, and say something like, "hello, my name is Mark."

If you want, you can ask someone you know to introduce you, but don't overcomplicate it. People make it too complicated. Just go over to them and introduce yourself. Simple.

Richard Lowe: Okay, then what??

Mark O'Donnell: I get the conversation going by saying something like, "tell me about your business and where do you think it's going?" That always gets someone talking.

Next, "How did you get to where you are today?"

Now, it's best to give them something, "Who could I introduce you to?" Usually that's a great way to get people to like you right way. You're offering to give them something and it's easy.

Finally, don't forget this one, "May I follow up with you? Do you prefer email, text or phone?" Always ask this. Some people use email, others like to be texted, but some hate it, and others want you to call.

Richard Lowe: I want people to email.

Mark O'Donnell: See? So, you ask. It's polite and it shows you respect them by communicating in the way they want.

Richard Lowe: Cool. I interviewed Ron Sukenick and he said one of the most important things about networking is that you give more than you receive. Would you say that's true, and, if so, why?

Mark O'Donnell: Absolutely. I think you must give without the expectation of receiving. It's sort of a karma concept. And I think it was Brian Tracey who said that the more people I help, the more people will help me.

It's like we have two ears and one mouth. I try to give twice as many referrals to my referral partners as I expect to receive back. I know, after doing this for so long, karma is good and the world of reciprocity is amazing.

There'll be days when I say, "Gosh, I really need to pound the pavement and fill my pipeline", and I have two or three people call me saying, "We have two people interested in joining."

The world of karma just sent me several strong referrals that I can then follow up, and see what questions they have about RGA. So, in answer to your question, I think that in life, anything worth doing is worth doing well.

Richard Lowe: I see how it works. You've talked about RGA a little bit, how about telling me more about why you started RGA and where it came from?

Mark O'Donnell: I've always been a big fan of connecting. At the museum, it was very important, when you were restoring cars, or trains or planes, to get the right, passionate professional to do the restoration.

You can be an auto body repair shop, but if you don't know how to work with fiberglass, for instance, then a lot of the corvettes wouldn't be your forte in restoring, and if you don't know how to work with a material, you're probably not going to be as passionate about it as someone who is a fanatic about sports cars.

It's the same way with networking. Connecting people has always been my passion. I did it in the museum by connecting vendors. If we had a good souvenir, I could call the Zoo and tell them, "I'm sending over this manufacturer's representative because they have great pricing on children's t-shirts and souvenir pencils. Would you be willing to see him if he stops by?"

Ninety-nine times out of a hundred they would see the representative as a personal favor to me.

Bonus: Interview with Mark O'Donnell

When I moved to Florida I looked at a lot of networking opportunities such as the Chambers of Commerce and seat-specific networking groups, meaning there's only one plumber, one hair salon, one pest control.

There are groups where networking kind of feels like a second job, where if you miss a meeting they kick you out, if you have no referrals they kick you out, if you're late they slap your hand, and sort of embarrass you, so it really felt like a second job.

Then there was a free group, and those people would come and go as they saw fit; I never felt like I got a significant referral passed to me. What I felt was that these people were trying to sell me or recruit me to sell their products or services, which is kind of a far stretch of networking – that's not why we're there.

We're there to promote our businesses. So, one day I decided that we could create a happy median of a networking group where we don't have to be seat-exclusive, where we don't have to require attendance, and I think if you provide value to the members they are going to show up and bring referrals with them.

I always say to people, "The best way to get a referral is to give a referral." Because it's part of human nature to pass it forward. In other words, if I do something nice for you, you'll pass it along to the next person.

Sometimes the universe seems to have a scoreboard; if you've done 10 nice things, the universe is going to reward you by people doing nice actions to you.

That's how RGA was born.

We were sitting there, watching these other poor people who, they didn't bring a referral,

For example, one lady was late because her daycare didn't open on time and she had to sit and wait because she couldn't leave her children alone.

When she arrived at the meeting late, they humiliated her by passing the "late arrival coffee can" and she had to come up with $3.50.

Her morning already wasn't going well. She got to the daycare, it wasn't open, she had to wait for them, she had to drop off her kids, then she saw some poor lady on the side of the street, reached into her purse and pulled out her only five, and gave it to the lady.

Then she gets to the networking meeting and not only is she humiliated for arriving late, but she had to give $3.50 to the coffee can. She couldn't because she, "Just gave it to this lady side of the road, who said she needed it to feed her family."

Richard Lowe: That would be the last time I attended that meeting.

Mark O'Donnell: It was the last time she attended. You want to help, I hope RGA creates an environment where people really want to help each other.

Bonus: Interview with Mark O'Donnell

Mark O'Donnell: These organizations, they have many strengths. One of the powers in making it mandatory to attend is you get the people who are very dedicated to the group.

For example, the lady we were just talking about, she was dedicated to the group. It was just the combination of bad events that all happened in one day; she had to borrow five dollars from somebody to pay the $3.50 fine, because the lady who opened the daycare center was late due to an emergency.

Instead of saying, "We are so glad you're here, we were worried about you, usually you're never late." Instead, it was "you owe a fine because you were late."

Richard Lowe: Okay, now describe a typical RGA meeting.

Mark O'Donnell: We wanted to do something different. So, when we first started, this whole concept was newly created and not practiced here in the Tampa Bay market.

Since then, people have copied our format, so I guess it's a form of flattery. The team leaders arrive early so they can get up and greet and introduce themselves to the new arrivals, especially first-timers. We want them to feel very welcome.

The meeting usually begins with, "Why we RGA." It's what makes us come back week after week, after week. A lot of people say they RGA because of the flexibility, they RGA because they can go to any meeting in the area, they can present their business to the RGA members at every one of our chapters.

We have a world-class website; it's 99.99% Google verified, meaning Google will trust the content from our website, along with our business directories. We are often able to get our members on the first page of Google under the categories they choose, which is huge for attorneys, writers, pest control, things that have a lot of competition. Those people know, if you are on the third page, nobody goes to page 3.

Our meeting agenda is standardized throughout our chapters, so if you attend a meeting you will experience the same order of things. It is structured but still allows for some flexibility on the part of the chapter directors. One thing we encourage during the meeting is for our members to have MOMs and DADS. We have our own language in RGA. MOM means meetings outside of meetings. DAD is discussions after dinner.

We encourage our members to meet outside meetings so they can get to know one another and to understand what makes them tick.

This goes back to that "like, know, and trust" factor. For example, if you meet somebody and you know that their business is the sole supporter of their household, they are probably going to be very serious about it.

I think having MOMs and DADs is crucial to the success of the network. People will say, "Richard does that, you really need to have a MOM with him. He just doesn't do coloring books".

Bonus: Interview with Mark O'Donnell

Richard Lowe: Tell me more about a MOM and how it should work.

Mark O'Donnell: A MOM should work – other organizations call them one-on-ones – we like to be a little more creative. These meetings are to get to know each other.

I want to find out what led you to where you're at now. Why are you in advertising, a sales person, or in talk media, and what got you to this level.

How many brothers and sisters do you have? Where did you grow up? What is more important to you, work or home life? You might be sitting across from the next Bill Gates or Warren Buffett, or Vera Wang. The only way you're going to know that is by asking questions.

"I work in advertising but my passion is I make all my own clothes."

You say, "What?"

"I make all my own clothes. I really want to be a designer in New York."

Now you are armed with more information. It is to get to know people on a deeper level. I ask, "How do you like to have your referrals passed on? Do you want me to call you, text you, email you? What is the best way for me to get you contact information of people who want you to reach out to them?"

I also explain my process. If I send you a referral, they know about you and are either expecting your call, or if the person doesn't feel comfortable with that, I give them your contact information so you know that they're supposed to call you.

Often, I try to get their cell phone number, because if you get a call from a cell phone, at least for me, and I don't recognize it, I let it go to voicemail so I can see what the person wants. But if you know that that is the number of the referral you are going to pick up.

Richard Lowe: Contrast a good MOM with a bad one.

Mark O'Donnell: A good MOM is where we get to know each other. We talk about where we're from, how many brothers and sisters we had, what kind of pets we had, what makes us tick, why do we get up in the morning and do what we do. Knowing people's lives is critically important.

Just to earn money is a good why, if you are earning money so your little kids can follow you in the path of attending an Ivy League school, you know that that person is really going to work.

They also ask questions about how they can help you. A good MOM goes both ways. You split the time, be it 30 minutes or an hour. For 15 minutes, they talk about themselves, for the other 15 minutes they ask you questions.

A bad MOM is when someone comes with both their sales brochure and their laptop, and they begin with their sales presentation on why their product or service or whatever is going to help you.

Bonus: Interview with Mark O'Donnell

A lot of networkers say that this is the best way for them to explain what they do. I've never found one of them at the end that closes the laptop and says, "Do you know anybody that that would help?"

They usually always ask me is this something I'd like to do. And then I say, "Really, we are not here to sell each other, you're here to educate me so when I am out working with somebody and they say, 'I'm not feeling very well, I wake up with a stiff neck all the time.' I say, 'oh my gosh, I found somebody who has a product that is specifically for people to wake up at stiff necks. Let me give you her name and number and you give them a quick call'."

That is a bad MOM, if they try to sell you. And sometimes if I'm interested in a product or service I'll say right then, "Pull out your calendar, I'm interested, but today's meeting is just for us to get to know each other. So, I would like to see what you can do from me, but because I'm usually time constrained, I don't have the time to extend my MOM by another 30 minutes or an hour."

Richard Lowe: Let's say you meet someone and he's in business and he's not a member of RGA, what do you tell him to get him interested in joining?

Mark O'Donnell: What I say to a lot of the people I meet, is that I represent some of the finest business owners in the area and I would love to invite you to a breakfast or lunch or whatever, or one of our happy hour meetings.

"I think these people are good business connections that can only help you in your business. I sometimes say that I'm in a networking group and there is not a problem in business that we cannot solve collectively. I'd love to connect you to my partners.

What day of the week are you typically free to meet for lunch?" And if they are free on a day that our chapter is a distance away, I offer to come by and pick them up so we can have a conversation while driving to the chapter that is far away.

I always say to people, "You must strive for consistency." I used to do stupid little puns, like, "Networking is a lot like Catholicism. You must show up for mass to get the full facts. If you want to be liked and known, you should be a regular at the meetings.

You can miss a few meetings here and there, most people will say, 'gosh is everything okay? We missed you last week.' But if you consistently go to one of the chapter's, people at another chapter would say the same thing."

Richard Lowe: One of the things that always gives me trouble is when you get a reference that you don't particularly want. You are not interested in following up with this person because it's not the kind of business you want to do, or they are not the kind of people you want to do business with. How do you handle that?

Mark O'Donnell: What I say is, "I really appreciate you thinking of me but that isn't really a fit from me, there is probably someone else in the RGA that could really utilize that referral to its fullest opportunity."

Bonus: Interview with Mark O'Donnell

Richard Lowe: For example, I don't do resumes. That's not something I can do well, and I get a lot of those and I really don't know how to say, "Sorry, this is not what I want to do."

Mark O'Donnell: When you are out networking, find someone who is good at writing resumes and say, "I get asked a lot to do resumes, would you have any problem with me sending you the people I get for resumes? How do you want me to do that? You want me to email you, only to give you a text, how so you want me to connect you?"

Then if they say, "Yes that's great, what can I do for you?" "Well, you know I'm very good at LinkedIn profiles, I'd appreciate you passing your LinkedIn profiles to me. Or, if you come across one that stumps you, then send it to me. I also do ghost blogging; every business owner needs a ghost blogger."

Then you say, "Resumes aren't really my thing, but this person is really good." My other advice is to stay organized, and use your time effectively. I think the networking meetings are very important, you get to see a lot of people in a short amount of time.

But when you schedule these MOMs, schedule them before or after the meeting. A lot of people will say, "Let's do 3 o'clock at Starbucks." Well, you have already blocked the time either for breakfast or lunch, maximize your time opportunities and do it right after the meeting or right before it.

Then follow up, follow up, follow up. As simple as, "Thanks for seeing me today, I learned a lot of great information. You can text that, email that, all those things are very acceptable forms these days."

But follow up. Because then you know that they have got your information. What I try to do is send a week later a more formal follow-up.

I always try in the next 30 days, to get them some sort of result from a meeting. An article I thought you might enjoy, an informational news clip, or something of the web, or a referral. It plants the seed.

I like to think of networking more like farming, rather than hunting. If you need a sale to feed your family by Friday, go hunting and make a sale. But if you want to cultivate a garden of ongoing, continuous referrals, you need to network.

The thing is, and I'm a farmer by nature – you can't just plant seeds, water them, and then walk away. You have to come back to make sure the seeds have sprouted, if they are vining beans you have to make sure there are poles for them, if it's carrots you have to make sure the stalks are growing right and that they are getting enough nutrition. But once you do, the harvest just keeps coming and coming. The abundances there if you work it.

Richard Lowe: That brings us to the end of the interview. Do you have any closing words?

Mark O'Donnell: I always say to people that you are the five people you surround yourself with, and the more people you surround yourself with, the more people you can connect with. We may be born alone and we may die alone, but we travelled

Bonus: Interview with Mark O'Donnell

the journey called life with other human beings. So, surround yourself with positive, like-minded individuals and cast your net for more business. Networking works when you work it, and I always tell people to network abundantly.

About the Author

https://www.linkedin.com/in/richardlowejr
Feel free to send a connection request

Follow me on Twitter: @richardlowejr

Richard Lowe has leveraged more than 35 years of experience as a Senior Computer Manager and Designer at four companies into that of a bestselling author, blogger, ghostwriter, and public speaker. He has written hundreds of articles for blogs and ghostwritten more than a dozen books and has published manuscripts about computers, the Internet, surviving disasters, management, and human rights. He is currently working on a ten-volume science fiction series – the Peacekeeper Series – to be published at the rate of three volumes per year, beginning in 2016.

Richard started in the field of Information Technology, first as the Vice President of Consulting at Software Techniques, Inc. Because he craved action, after six years he moved on to work for two companies at the same time: he was the Vice President of Consulting at Beck Computer Systems and the Senior Designer at BIF Accutel. In January 1994, Richard found a home at Trader Joe's as the Director of Technical Services and Computer Operations. He remained with that incredible company for almost 20 years before taking an early retirement to begin a new life as a professional writer. He is currently the CEO of The Writing King, a company that provides all forms of writing services, the owner of The EBay King, and a Senior Branding Expert for LinkedIn Makeover. You can find a current list of all books on his Author Page and

About the Author

take a look at his exclusive line of coloring books at The Coloring King.

Richard has a quirky sense of humor and has found that life is full of joy and wonder. As he puts it, "This little ball of rock, mud, and water we call Earth is an incredible place, with many secrets to discover. Beings fill our corner of the universe, and some are happy, and others are sad, but each has their unique story to tell."

His philosophy is to take life with a light heart, and he approaches each day as a new source of happiness. Evil is ignored, discarded, or defeated; good is helped, enriched, and fulfilled. One of his primary interests is to educate people about their human rights and assist them to learn how to be happy in life.

Richard spent many happy days hiking in national parks, crawling over boulders, and peering at Indian pictographs. He toured the Channel Islands off Santa Barbara and stared in fascination at wasps building their homes in Anza-Borrego. One of his joys is photography, and he has photographed more than 1,200 belly dancing events, as well as dozens of Renaissance fairs all over the country.

Because writing is his passion, Richard remains incredibly creative and prolific; each day he writes between 5,000 and 10,000 words, diligently using language to bring life to the world so that others may learn and be entertained.

Richard is the CEO of The Writing King, which specializes in fulfilling any writing need. You can find out more at https://www.thewritingking.com/, and emails are welcome at rich@thewritingking.com

Books by Richard G Lowe Jr.

Business Professional Series

On the Professional Code of Ethics and Business Conduct in the Workplace – Professional Ethics: 100 Tips to Improve Your Professional Life - have you ever wondered what it takes to be successful in the professional world? This book gives you some tips that will improve your job and your career.

Help! My Boss is Whacko! - How to Deal with a Hostile Work Environment - sometimes the problem is the boss. There are all kinds of managers, some competent, some incompetent, and others just plain whacked. This book will help you understand and handle those different types of managers.

Help! I've Lost My Job: Tips on What to do When You're Unexpectedly Unemployed – suddenly having to leave your job can be a harsh and emotional time in your life. Learn some of the things that you need to consider and handle if this happens to you.

Help! My Job Sucks Insider Tips on Making Your Job More Satisfying and Improving Your Career – sometimes conditions conspire to make the regular trek to a job feel like a trip through Dante's Inferno. Sometimes, these are out of our control, such as a malicious manager or incompetent colleague. On the other hand, we can take control of our lives and workplace and improve our situation. Get this book to learn what you can do when your job sucks.

Books by Richard G Lowe Jr.

How to Manage a Consulting Project: Make money, get your project done on time, and get referred again and again – I found that being a consultant is a great way to earn a living. Managing a consulting project can be a challenge. This book contains some tips to help you so you can deliver a better product or service to your customers.

How to be a Good Manager and Supervisor, and How to Delegate – Lessons Learned from the Trenches: Insider Secrets for Managers and Supervisors – I've been a manager for over thirty years I learned many things about how to get the job done and deliver quality service. The information in this book will help you manage your projects to a high level of quality.

Focus on LinkedIn – Learn how to create a LinkedIn profile and to network effectively using the #1 business social media site.

Home Computer Security Series

Safe Computing is Like Safe Sex: You have to practice it to avoid infection – Security expert and Computer Executive, Richard Lowe, presents the simple steps you can take to protect your computer, photos and information from evil doers and viruses. Using easy-to-understand examples and simple explanations, Lowe explains why hackers want your system, what they do with your information, and what you can do to keep them at bay. Lowe answers the question: how to you keep yourself say in the wild west of the internet.

Books by Richard G Lowe Jr.

Disaster Preparation and Survival Series

Real World Survival Tips and Survival Guide: Preparing for and Surviving Disasters with Survival Skills – CERT (Civilian Emergency Response Team) trained and Disaster Recovery Specialist, Richard Lowe, lays out how to make you, your family, and your friends ready for any disaster, large or small. Based upon specialized training, interviews with experts and personal experience, Lowe answers the big question: what is the secret to improving the odds of survival even after a big disaster?

Creating a Bug Out Bag to Save Your Life: What you need to pack for emergency evacuations - When you are ordered to evacuate—or leave of your free will—you probably won't have a lot of time to gather your belongings and the things you'll need. You may have just a few minutes to get out of your home. The best preparation for evacuation is to create what is called a bug out bag. These are also known as go-bags, as in, "grab it and go!"

Professional Freelance Writer Series

How to Operate a Freelance Writing Business, and How to be a Ghostwriter – Proven Tips and Tricks Every Author Needs to Know about Freelance Writing: Insider Secrets from a Professional Ghostwriter – This book explains how to be a ghostwriter, and gives tips on everything from finding customers to creating a statement of work to delivering your final product.

How to Write a Blog That Sells and How to Make Money From Blogging: Insider Secrets from a Professional Blogger:

Books by Richard G Lowe Jr.

Proven Tips and Tricks Every Blogger Needs to Know to Make Money – There is an art to writing an article that prompts the reader to make a decision to do something. That's the narrow focus of this book. You will learn how to create an article that gets a reader interested, entices them, informs them, and causes them to make a decision when they reach the end.

<u>Other Books by Richard Lowe Jr</u>

<u>How to Be Friends with Women: How to Surround Yourself with Beautiful Women without Being Sleazy</u> – I am a photographer and frequently find myself surrounded by some of the most beautiful women in the world. This book explains how men can attract women and keep them as friends, which can often lead to real, fulfilling relationships.

<u>How to Throw Parties like a Professional: Tips to Help You Succeed with Putting on a Party Event</u> – Many of us have put on parties, and I know it can be a daunting and confusing experience. In this book, I share what I learned from hosting small house parties to shows and events.

Additional Resources

Is your career important to you? Find out how to move your career in any direction you desire, improve your long-term livelihood, and be prepared for any eventuality. Visit the page below to sign up to receive valuable tips via email, and to get a free eBook about how to optimize your LinkedIn profile.

http://list.thewritingking.com/

I've written and published many books on a variety of subjects. They are all listed on the following page.

https://www.thewritingking.com/books/

On that site, I also publish articles about business, writing, and other subjects. You can visit by clicking the following link:

https://www.thewritingking.com

To find out more about me or my photography, you can visit these sites:

Personal website: https://www.richardlowe.com
Photography: http://www.richardlowejr.com
LinkedIn Profile: https://www.linkedin.com/in/richardlowejr
Twitter: https://twitter.com/richardlowejr

If you have any comments about this book, feel free to email me at rich@thewritingking.com

Premium Writing Services

Do you have a story that needs to be told? Have you been trying to write a book for ages but never can seem to find the time to get it done? Do you want to brand your business, but don't know how to get started?

The Writing King has the answer. We can help you with any of your writing needs.

Ghostwriting. We can write your book, which entails interviewing you to get your story, writing the book and then working with you to revise it until complete. To discuss your book, contact The Writing King today.

Website Copy. Many businesses include the text on their sites as an afterthought, and that can result in lost sales and leads. Hire The Writing King to review your site and recommend changes to the text which will help communicate your message and improve your sales.

Blogging. Build engagement with your customers by hiring us to write a weekly or semi-weekly article for your blog, LinkedIn or other social media. Contact The Writing King today to discuss your blogging needs.

LinkedIn. LinkedIn is of the most important vehicles for finding new business, and a professionally written profile works to pulling in those leads. Write or update your profile today.

Technical Writing. We have broad experience in the computer, warehousing and retail industries, and have written hundreds of technical documents. Contact <u>The Writing King</u> today to find out how we can help you with your technical writing project.

<u>The Writing King</u> has the skills and knowledge to help you with any of your writing needs. Call us today to discuss how we can help you.